4th Grade

GEORGIA

ELA TEST PREP

Common Core State Standards

INTRODUCTION

Our 4th Grade ELA Test Prep for Common Core State Standards is an excellent resource to supplement your classroom's curriculum to assess and manage students' understanding of concepts outlined in the Common Core State Standards Initiative for Reading Literature and Reading Informational Text. There are several questions aligned to each Common Core Standard Reading Literature and Informational Text standard. We recommend the student read the story passage and answer the questions that follow each story in the book. The answers marked by the student can serve as a diagnostic tool to determine WHY the student had an incorrect answer. The answer to the student's misunderstanding is NOT another worksheet, but a re-teaching of the skill, using different instructional strategies.

The reason for incorrect answers is often the result of the student using an incorrect procedure. Most of the errors we see as teachers and parents are the same each year. Students apply a rule in an inappropriate way. Many times they will even say to us, "That's what you said to do." They see logic in the way they have applied the rule even though it is incorrect. Therefore, it is imperative to determine WHY a student chose an incorrect answer to a question. The best way to determine this is to ask the student to explain their reasoning to you.

All questions in this product are aligned to the current Common Core State Standards Initiative. To view the standards, refer to pages *i* through *iii*.

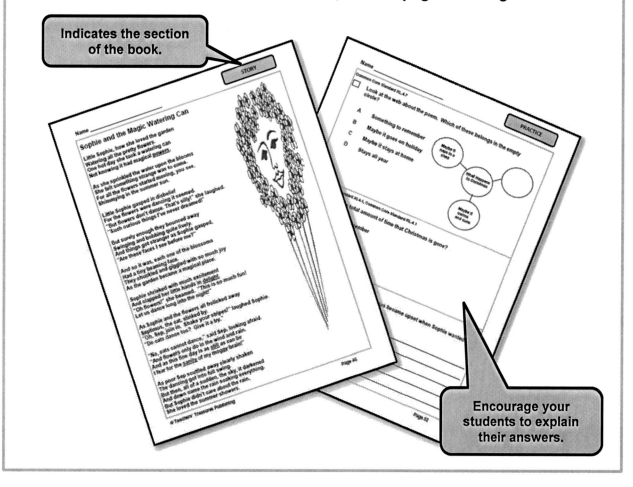

Indicates the section of the book.

Encourage your students to explain their answers.

4th Grade
ELA Test Prep
FOR
Common Core
Standards

Reading Literature - Key Ideas and Details   RL.4.1

Refer to details and examples in a text when explaining what the text says explicitly and when drawing inferences from the text.

Reading Literature – Key Ideas and Details   RL.4.2

Determine a theme of a story, drama, or poem from details in the text; summarize the text.

Reading Literature – Key Ideas and Details   RL.4.3

Describe in depth a character, setting, or event in a story or drama, drawing on specific details in the text (e.g., a character's thoughts, words, or actions).

Reading Literature – Craft and Structure   RL.4.4

Determine the meaning of words and phrases as they are used in a text, including those that allude to significant characters found in mythology (e.g., Herculean).

Reading Literature – Craft and Structure   RL.4.5

Explain major differences between poems, drama, and prose, and refer to the structural elements of poems (e.g., verse, rhythm, meter) and drama (e.g., casts of characters, settings, descriptions, dialogue, stage directions) when writing or speaking about a text.

Reading Literature – Craft and Structure   RL.4.6

Compare and contrast the point of view from which different stories are narrated, including the difference between first- and third-person narrations.

Reading Literature – Integration of Knowledge and Ideas   RL.4.7

Make connections between the text of a story or drama and a visual or oral presentation of the text, identifying where each version reflects specific descriptions and directions in the text.

Reading Literature – Integration of Knowledge and Ideas   RL.4.8

(RL.4.8 not applicable to literature)

Reading Literature – Integration of Knowledge and Ideas   RL.4.9

Compare and contrast the treatment of similar themes and topics (e.g., opposition of good and evil) and patterns of events (e.g., the quest) in stories, myths, and traditional literature from different cultures.

Reading Literature –Range of Reading and Level of Text Complexity · RL.4.10

By the end of the year, read and comprehend literature, including stories, dramas, and poetry, in the grades 4–5 text complexity band proficiently, with scaffolding as needed at the high end of the range.

Reading Informational Text – Key Ideas and Details · RI.4.1

Refer to details and examples in a text when explaining what the text says explicitly and when drawing inferences from the text.

Reading Informational Text – Key Ideas and Details · RI.4.2

Determine the main idea of a text and explain how it is supported by key details; summarize the text.

Reading Informational Text – Key Ideas and Details · RI.4.3

Explain events, procedures, ideas, or concepts in a historical, scientific, or technical text, including what happened and why, based on specific information in the text.

Reading Informational Text – Craft and Structure · RI.4.4

Determine the meaning of general academic and domain-specific words or phrases in a text relevant to a *grade 4 topic or subject area*.

Reading Informational Text – Craft and Structure · RI.4.5

Describe the overall structure (e.g., chronology, comparison, cause/effect, problem/solution) of events, ideas, concepts, or information in a text or part of a text.

Reading Informational Text – Craft and Structure · RI.4.6

Compare and contrast a firsthand and secondhand account of the same event or topic; describe the differences in focus and the information provided.

Reading Informational Text – Integration of Knowledge and Ideas · RI.4.7

Interpret information presented visually, orally, or quantitatively (e.g., in charts, graphs, diagrams, time lines, animations, or interactive elements on Web pages) and explain how the information contributes to an understanding of the text in which it appears.

Reading Informational Text – Integration of Knowledge and Ideas · RI.4.8

Explain how an author uses reasons and evidence to support particular points in a text.

Reading Informational Text – Integration of Knowledge and Ideas   RI.4.9

Integrate information from two texts on the same topic in order to write or speak about the subject knowledgeably.

Reading Informational Text – Range of Reading and Level of Text Complexity   RI.4.10

By the end of year, read and comprehend informational texts, including history/social studies, science, and technical texts, in the grades 4–5 text complexity band proficiently, with scaffolding as needed at the high end of the range.

The Laundry

"I know I'll mess it up!" Toby said. He and his mother were discussing his new household <u>tasks</u> now that Mrs. Duncan would be working at the mall five days a week. Mrs. Duncan told Toby that he would be responsible for doing the dishes and the laundry. Toby felt pretty confident that he could do the dishes. After all, anyone could put dirty dishes into the dishwasher, add soap, and turn it on. But the laundry was <u>entirely</u> different. If he did not put the right clothes together with the correct water temperature, the clothes could be ruined.

"I'll show you what to do. Don't worry," his mother said. "I know you'll do a good job."

Toby and his mother began the process of sorting the laundry into piles. His mother explained why each <u>article</u> of clothing belonged in that particular pile. Toby began to feel less <u>unsure</u> as he and his mother worked together. He knew the real test would come when he had to sort the laundry by himself.

"Why do you put all of the white clothes together?" Toby asked his mother.

"That's a good question," replied Mrs. Duncan. "Sometimes the dye in colored clothing will come off on the white ones. You don't want that to happen. You might <u>end up</u> with pink instead of white socks."

"What about towels?" asked Toby. "Do they need to be washed in cold or hot water?"

"I don't think you should use either one. I <u>prefer</u> for you to use warm water for the towels," his mother explained.

Toby looked at the piles of clothes. He wanted to help his mother, but he still was not certain he would be able to remember everything his mother had explained to him. Then he had an idea. What if he and his mother wrote on a piece of paper the directions for sorting the clothes, the water temperature, and the dryer temperature for each type of clothing he would be washing? When he told his mother his idea, they immediately began writing the set of instructions. When they finished, Toby taped the piece of paper to the cabinet door above the washing machine.

Here are the instructions Toby and his mother wrote.

TOBY'S LAUNDRY RULES

White Clothes
1. Check the pockets of all <u>garments</u> and <u>remove</u> anything you find.
2. Place the clothing <u>loosely</u> into the washer.
3. Add <u>detergent</u>. 1/2 cup for half a load, and 1 cup for a full load.
4. Wash on delicate cycle; cold water.
5. When cycle is completed, place clothing in dryer for 20 minutes on <u>delicate</u> cycle.

Colored Clothing
1. Check the pockets of all garments and remove anything you find.
2. Turn all of the pieces of clothing inside out.
3. Place the clothing loosely into the washer.
4. Add detergent. 1/2 cup for half a load, and 1 cup for a full load.
5. Wash on perma-press <u>cycle</u>; cold water.
6. When cycle is completed, place clothing in dryer for 20 minutes on perma-press cycle.

Towels
1. Place the towels loosely in the washer.
2. Add detergent. 1/2 cup for half a load, and 1 cup for a full load.
3. Wash on regular cycle; warm water.
4. When cycle is completed, place towels in dryer for 30 minutes on normal cycle.

Common Core Standard RI4.4

☐   In this passage, the word <u>tasks</u> means _____

    A   jobs

    B   appliances

    C   tools

    D   items

Common Core Standard RI.4.4;, Common Core Standard RL.4.4

☐   In this passage, the word <u>article</u> means ____

    A   story

    B   piece

    C   laundry

    D   part of speech

Common Core Standard RI.4.4

☐   In this passage, the word <u>entirely</u> means ____

    A   of different colors

    B   hopelessly

    C   completely

    D   not very much

Name _____

Common Core Standard RI.4.4;, Common Core Standard RL.4.4

☐   **In this passage, the words <u>end up</u> mean _____**

    A   bottom on the top

    B   finish with

    C   take off the top

    D   find

Common Core Standard RI.4.4

☐   **In this passage, the word <u>garments</u> means _____**

    A   white shirts

    B   new jackets

    C   sheets

    D   pieces of clothing

Common Core Standard RI.4.4

☐   **In this passage, the word <u>loosely</u> means _____**

    A   not packed tightly

    B   arranged evenly

    C   in layers

    D   with similar colors

Common Core Standard RI.4.4; Common Core Standard RL.4.4

☐ In this passage, the word <u>delicate</u> means _____

A   used for soft, thin fabrics

B   lacy

C   used for old clothing

D   used for new clothing

Common Core Standard RI.4.4

☐ In this passage, the word <u>detergent</u> means _____

A   water softener

B   rinse

C   soap

D   clothing

Common Core Standard RI.4.4, Common Core Standard RL.4.4

☐ In this passage, the word <u>cycle</u> means _____

A   something to ride on

B   easy to do

C   washing machine

D   sequence of actions

Name _____

Common Core Standard RI.4.4

☐   **In this passage, the word <u>unsure</u> means _____**

     A   not certain

     B   confident

     C   curious

     D   helpless

Common Core Standard RI.4.4

☐   **In this passage, the word <u>prefer</u> means _____**

     A   worried about

     B   like better

     C   disappointed

     D   seen often

Common Core Standard RI.4.4

☐   **In this passage, the word <u>remove</u> means _____**

     A   go to another place

     B   put together

     C   easy to do

     D   take away

Common Core Standard RI.4.3

☐ **What did Toby and his mother do after they finished writing the laundry instructions?**

A   Began sorting the laundry

B   Taped the paper to the cabinet door

C   Turned on the washing machine

D   Put the clothes in the dryer

Common Core Standard RI.4.3

☐ **What should Toby do before he adds detergent to the washing machine?**

A   Select the water temperature

B   Turn on the washing machine

C   Place the items in the washer

D   Put the items in the dryer

Common Core Standard RI.4.3

☐ **Which of these happened first in this passage?**

A   Toby and his mother wrote instructions for doing the laundry.

B   They placed a piece of paper on the cabinet door.

C   The laundry was placed in the washer.

D   They sorted the laundry into piles.

Name _____

☐ Why did Toby's mother say not to put white and colored clothing in the same pile?

A   They will get mixed up.

B   All clothing should be put in piles for each different color.

C   The dye in colored clothing can sometimes get on the white clothing.

D   No one wants pink socks.

☐ Why should towels not be washed with white clothes?

A   Towels are larger.

B   Towels should be washed on the regular cycle.

C   There are more towels than white clothing.

D   Towels need more detergent than white clothing.

☐ Why did Toby's mother need his help with some of the household jobs?

A   She would be working at the mall.

B   She wanted him to do more jobs than he had been doing.

C   She did not like to do the laundry.

D   These were easy jobs that he could do.

Common Core Standard RI.4.1

☐ Where were Toby and his mother when they were sorting the laundry into piles?

A   At Toby's school

B   At the mall

C   In Toby's bedroom

D   At Toby's house

Common Core Standard RI.4.1

☐ Where did Toby put the set of laundry instructions?

A   In the bathroom

B   Above the washing machine

C   In the kitchen

D   On the bedroom door

Common Core Standard RI.4.1

☐ When will Toby use the instructions?

A   On Tuesdays

B   When his mother helps him

C   When he does the laundry

D   On his birthday

Common Core Standard RI.4.7

☐ **Which type of clothing should be washed in warm water?**

A   Colored

B   Towels

C   White

D   Old

Common Core Standard RI.4.9

☐ **Which two kinds of clothing need to be dried for 20 minutes?**

A   White and towels

B   Towels and colored

C   White and new

D   Colored and white

Common Core Standard RI.4.7

☐ **What kind of clothing should be washed on the perma-press cycle?**

A   Colored

B   White

C   Towels

D   White and colored

Common Core Standard RI.4.2

☐ **What is the main idea of this passage?**

A   Toby is afraid to do the laundry by himself.

B   Toby's mom is starting a new job at the mall.

C   Toby's mother helps him learn how to do the laundry.

D   The instructions are taped to the cabinet door.

Common Core Standard RI.4.2

☐ **What is the main idea of the laundry rules?**

A   Colored clothes should be washed in cold water.

B   They tell how to wash and dry different kinds of clothing.

C   There are three kinds of clothing.

D   Towels and white clothing are the most difficult to wash.

Common Core Standard RI.4.2

☐ **The main idea of this passage is how to _____**

A   write instructions

B   help your mom

C   do household tasks

D   do laundry correctly

Name _____

Common Core Standard RL.4.2

☐ **What is this passage mostly about?**

A   A boy and his mom write directions for doing the laundry so that he can help with some of the housework now that his mom will be working at the mall.

B   A boy and his mom write directions for washing towels and put them on the cabinet door.

C   A boy's mom helps him put the dirty clothes into piles.

D   Even though a boy wants to help his mom with household tasks, he does not believe he can remember how to do the laundry.

Common Core Standard RL.4.2

☐ **In "Toby's Laundry Rules," what is the section *Colored Clothing* mostly about?**

A   Colored clothing should be washed in cold water on the delicate cycle and dried for 20 minutes.

B   Colored clothing should be washed in cold water using one cup of detergent.

C   When washing colored clothing, you should turn the clothes inside out, wash in cold water on perma-press cycle, and dry for 20 minutes.

D   When washing colored clothing, you should place the clothing loosely in the washer, use cold water, and dry for 20 minutes on the delicate cycle.

Common Core Standard RL.4.2

☐ **What is the first paragraph in this passage mostly about?**

A   Toby's mother is going to work at the mall five days a week.

B   Toby's mother wants him to help with some of the housework, but he is not sure he knows how to do the laundry.

C   Toby and his mother discuss his new responsibilities and write a set of instructions for doing the laundry.

D   Toby's mother will help him put the clothes in piles.

Common Core Standard RI.4.1

☐ Toby will need to help his mother with some of the household tasks because ____

A   his mother thinks it is time that he learns to do the laundry

B   his mother will not have time to do some of the jobs

C   he is receiving an allowance for helping around the house

D   all of his friends have chores

Common Core Standard RI.4.1

☐ Toby and his mother wrote a list of instructions for doing the family laundry because ____

A   he was not listening when his mother explained the job to him

B   his mother does not think he can do a good job without instructions

C   he did not think he could remember everything his mother had told him

D   he had a homework assignment to do

Common Core Standard RI.4.1, Common Core Standard RL.4.3

☐ Why was Toby worried about doing the family laundry?

A   He knew his mother would get mad if he made a mistake.

B   He would not have time to play baseball after school if he did household chores.

C   Doing the laundry was the most difficult job of all.

D   He was afraid he would ruin some of their clothes.

Name _____

Common Core Standard Rl.4.5, Common Core Standard RL.4.3

☐   **Which of the following is most likely to happen in the future?**

    A   Toby's mother will start doing the laundry again.

    B   Toby will ruin most of their clothes.

    C   Toby will cook the dinner each evening.

    D   Toby will not need to look at the instructions when he does the laundry.

Common Core Standard Rl.4.5, Common Core Standard RL.4.3

☐   **Toby probably wanted his mother to help him write the instructions for doing the laundry because he _____**

    A   could look at them if he forgot how to sort certain items

    B   knew she did not trust him to do a good job

    C   did not want to listen to her instructions

    D   could do the laundry much faster

Common Core Standard Rl.4.5

☐   **What could probably cause some white socks to turn pink?**

    A   Toby might put some pink dye in the washer.

    B   Toby might put some white socks and a red shirt in the washer.

    C   Toby's mother could trick Toby.

    D   The washer might quit working.

Common Core Standard RI.4.5, Common Core Standard RL.4.9

☐ **Why did Toby's mother probably agree to help him write a set of laundry instructions?**

A   She liked to write instructions for Toby.

B   It would make him more confident.

C   Toby never remembered anything she told him.

D   She did not want to ever do the laundry again.

Common Core Standard RL.4.3

☐ **Mrs. Duncan is certain that Toby will do a good job, but Toby _____**

A   thinks it is a job for girls

B   does not want to do the laundry

C   is afraid he will make a mistake

D   would rather be outside playing with his friends

Common Core Standard RI.4.5, Common Core Standard RL.4.3

☐ **Toby thinks washing the dishes is easier because _____**

A   there are fewer steps to do

B   he has watched his mother

C   they are smaller than clothes

D   you do not need to add detergent

Common Core Standard RI.4.8

☐ The reader can tell that _____

A   Toby thinks his mother should do the household tasks

B   Toby wants to help his mother

C   Mrs. Duncan is asking Toby to do too much

D   Toby will make a mistake

Common Core Standard RI.4.8

☐ The reader can tell that when Toby asks his mother to help him write the laundry instructions, he _____

A   thinks this job is too hard

B   wishes she would tell him he does not have to do the laundry

C   is delaying the job

D   does not want to disappoint his mother

Common Core Standard RI.4.8

☐ Information in the passage suggests that _____

A   Toby's mother will not work at the mall for very long

B   Toby will ask his sister to do these jobs

C   Toby has never done the dishes or washed clothes

D   Mrs. Duncan is not sure Toby can handle these jobs

Name _____

Common Core Standard RL.4.3

☐ **Which of these words best describes Toby?**

A   Spoiled

B   Nosey

C   Famous

D   Trustworthy

Common Core Standard RL.4.3

☐ **The first time Toby does the laundry without his mother's help, he will probably feel ____**

A   Confident

B   Nervous

C   Curious

D   Silly

Common Core Standard RL.4.3

☐ **Why did Mrs. Duncan tell Toby that she knew he would do a good job?**

A   She wanted to make sure he tried.

B   She did not care if he did a good job or not.

C   She wanted him to know that she had confidence in him.

D   She was worried he would ruin their clothes.

Common Core Standard RL.4.3

☐ You can tell from this passage that Toby believes he will _____

A use the instructions when he does the family laundry

B ruin all of their clothes

C break all of the dishes

D lose the instructions sheet

Common Core Standard RL.4.3

☐ The passage suggests that _____

A Mrs. Duncan is glad she will be working

B Toby is afraid of his mother

C Toby's mother understands how he feels

D Mrs. Duncan does not care if Toby makes a mistake when sorting the laundry

Common Core Standard RL.4.9

☐ What could happen that would cause a problem for Toby?

A Mrs. Duncan might forget how to do the laundry.

B Toby might lose the instruction sheet.

C Toby might have only towels to wash.

D Mrs. Duncan might quit her job.

Name _____

Common Core Standard RI.4.3, Common Core Standard RI.4.7

☐ **Why do the laundry instructions say to use 1/2 cup of detergent for half a load?**

A   The clothes are not very dirty.

B   It does not take as much soap to do half a load as it does to do a full load.

C   It does not take as much soap when you are using cold water.

D   Mrs. Duncan is trying to save detergent.

Common Core Standard RI.4.3

☐ **Why does it usually take longer to dry towels than white clothes?**

A   Towels are made from thicker cloth.

B   Towels are different colors.

C   People use more towels in a week.

D   White clothes are harder to iron.

Common Core Standard RI.4.3

☐ **Why do the instructions probably say to place the clothing loosely in the washer?**

A   To keep them from getting wrinkled

B   To use less detergent

C   So they will not fade

D   So they will wash completely

Common Core Standard RL.4.3

☐ The steps are probably numbered in the laundry instructions so that ____

A   Mrs. Duncan can read them easier

B   Toby can follow them in order

C   Toby can use them for a homework assignment

D   Toby's sister can do the laundry

Common Core Standard RL.4.3

☐ Toby and his mother probably did not include instructions for washing the dishes because ____

A   Toby will wash more clothes than dishes

B   Toby's sister will wash the dishes

C   they will do those instructions later

D   Toby knows how to wash the dishes

Common Core Standard RL.4.3

☐ Toby should check the pockets of clothes before he washes them because ____

A   they will be washed in cold water

B   they are not very dirty

C   objects can be ruined in the washing machine

D   he might find a valuable coin

Common Core Standard RI.4.6, Common Core Standard RL.4.1

☐ **Which of these is a FACT in this passage?**

A   Toby was confident he knew how to wash the dishes.

B   Toby taped the set of instructions to the door.

C   Mrs. Duncan knew Toby would do a good job.

D   Mrs. Duncan thought Toby had asked good questions.

Common Core Standard RI.4.6, Common Core Standard RL.4.1

☐ **Which of these is an OPINION in this passage?**

A   Toby and his mother wrote instructions to help Toby with the laundry.

B   Toby was to be responsible for washing the dishes and doing the family laundry.

C   The instructions included the dryer temperature for different kinds of clothing.

D   Mrs. Duncan told Toby she knew he would do a good job.

Common Core Standard RI.4.6, Common Core Standard RL.4.1

☐ **Which of these is a FACT in this passage?**

A   Toby and his mother sorted the laundry into piles.

B   Toby knew that he would mess up.

C   Mrs. Duncan will be working at the mall four days a week.

D   Anyone can put dirty dishes into the dishwasher.

Common Core Standard RL.4.7

[ ]   The author probably wrote this passage to _____

    A   teach boys how to do laundry

    B   describe how to write instructions

    C   entertain the reader

    D   give an opinion

Common Core Standard RL.4.7

[ ]   The author probably wrote the set of instructions so that _____

    A   the reader could learn how to write instructions

    B   the reader could learn how to do laundry

    C   he would be famous

    D   he could describe clothing

Common Core Standard RL.4.7

[ ]   The author of this passage probably has _____

    A   a child that does the family laundry

    B   a wife that works in the mall

    C   lots of dirty clothes

    D   washed dishes and clothes

Common Core Standard RL.4.6

☐ The author of this passage probably believes ____

A everyone should do the dishes

B mothers should work in the mall

C children should have chores

D Toby will ruin all of their clothes

Common Core Standard RL.4.6

☐ The author of this passage is probably trying to show that ____

A washing dishes and doing laundry are not just jobs for girls

B Toby and his mother are angry at each other

C Mrs. Duncan should not ask Toby to do household jobs

D everyone should write instructions for their children

Common Core Standard RL.4.6

☐ The author of this passage probably wants the readers to ____

A dislike Toby

B respect Toby

C think Toby is not responsible

D dislike Mrs. Duncan

Nellie Bly: A Traveling Hero

t was the fall of 1888. A young reporter who signed her newspaper stories as Nellie Bly, but whose real name was Elizabeth Cochrane, approached her editor, John Cockerill, one Monday morning with a <u>unique</u> idea. Everyone seemed to be talking about a new book, *Around the World in Eighty Days,* by Jules Verne. She suggested that if she could go around the world in less than eighty days, it would make a fascinating story. She <u>convinced</u> Mr. Cockerill that if he allowed her to do this, she would send back stories of her race against time.

Her editor thought it was an idea worth considering, but he was not sure that a woman could accomplish this. After all, Nellie was only twenty-two. However, she had gone to prisons, insane asylums, and mines to get stories, so this was not that <u>unusual</u> for her. She told her editor that if he sent a man and not her, she would start the race on the same day for another newspaper and beat the man.

The editor had learned something about Nellie. When she made up her mind to do something, it was almost impossible to <u>discourage</u> her. Her <u>threat</u> had not fallen on deaf ears. He decided it was <u>useless</u> to argue any more.

Three days later, Nellie Bly set sail from Hoboken Pier in New York on a <u>liner</u> named the Augusta Victoria. She carried only one piece of hand luggage for the journey. It was just 16 inches wide and 7 inches high. She had managed to <u>squeeze</u> all that she thought she would need into the small bag.

The next day, her newspaper, *The World*, had a big story about the girl reporter who was going to try to beat the hero of the <u>novel</u> and go around the world in less than eighty days. Readers were interested at once. In a little over six days, her ship arrived in England.

As soon as she landed, she <u>cabled</u> a story to New York. Then she rushed for the train in London to take her on the next <u>leg</u> of her journey. She traveled across France and down to Italy, sending back a story at every stop. Then she boarded a ship to sail eastward across the Mediterranean Sea.

By now, thousands of readers in America were looking at maps, following the route of Nellie Bly. Each day they read the latest news of how she rode a donkey through Port Said and how hot it was at the Suez Canal. She also wrote of the mountains, rivers, temples, camels, elephants, and jewels that she had seen. From Canton, China, Nellie wrote that she had bought a monkey that sat on her shoulder. Finally, she was in Japan and boarding the ship that would take her across the Pacific to America.

A fierce storm occurred at sea, but Nellie only worried about the delay. The days of traveling were adding up, but finally the ship docked at San Francisco. Everyone cheered as the slender girl with a monkey on her shoulder got off the ship. Nellie <u>boarded</u> a special train that would carry her across the country. People gathered at stations to see the train that was carrying Nellie Bly.

At last, the train pulled into New York. Nellie Bly had traveled almost twenty-five thousand miles. She had gone around the world in seventy-two days, six hours, and eleven minutes. She had broken the record of the book, and she was the most famous woman on earth.

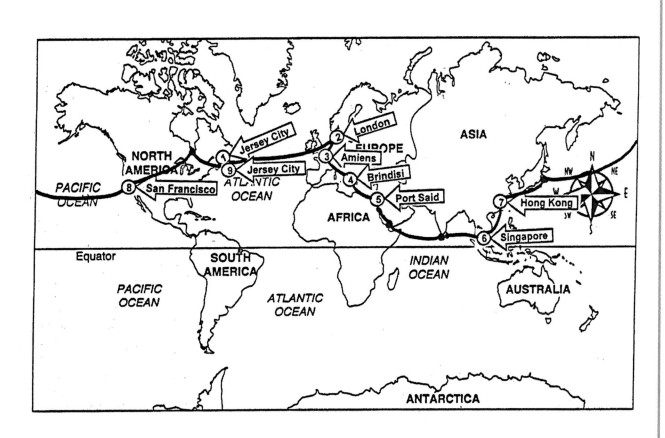

Common Core Standard RI4.4

☐ In this passage, the word <u>unique</u> means _____

A   wonderful

B   unusual

C   boring

D   friendly

Common Core Standard RI.4.4

☐ In this passage, the word <u>convinced</u> means _____

A   talked into something

B   threatened

C   is easy to believe

D   has many reasons

Common Core Standard RI4.4; RL.4.4

☐ In this passage, the word <u>threat</u> means _____

A   idea

B   secret

C   warning

D   story

Common Core Standard RI.4.4, Common Core Standard RL.4.4

☐   **In this passage, the word <u>liner</u> means _____**

A   airplane

B   carriage

C   piece of paper

D   ship

Common Core Standard RI.4.4; RL.4.4

☐   **In this passage, the word <u>squeeze</u> means _____**

A   hug tightly

B   wash with cleaner

C   crowd into a small package

D   pack

Common Core Standard RI4.4, Common Core Standard RL.4.4

☐   **In this passage, the word <u>novel</u> means _____**

A   interesting

B   book

C   journey

D   newspaper article

Common Core Standard RI.4.4, Common Core Standard RL.4.4

☐   **In this passage, the word <u>cabled</u> means _____**

A   talked to

B   asked for

C   sent

D   wanted

Common Core Standard RI.4.4, Common Core Standard RL.4.4

☐   **In this passage, the word <u>leg</u> means _____**

A   part of a trip

B   part of a table

C   part of a person's body

D   going from place to place

Common Core Standard RI.4.4, Common Core Standard RL.4.4

☐   **In this passage, the word <u>boarded</u> means _____**

A   located

B   got off

C   saw

D   got on

Common Core Standard RI.4.4

☐   In this passage, the word <u>unusual</u> means _____

    A   easy

    B   different

    C   like a lady

    D   hopeless

Common Core Standard RI.4.4

☐   In this passage, the word <u>discourage</u> means _____

    A   paid a lot of money

    B   easy to understand

    C   worried about

    D   talk out of doing something

Common Core Standard RI.4.4

☐   In this passage, the word <u>useless</u> means _____

    A   used a lot

    B   not touched

    C   not useful

    D   not real

Common Core Standard RL4.1

☐ **What did Nellie Bly need to do before she could go on the trip?**

A   Pack several large bags with clothing

B   Read <u>Around the World in Eighty Days</u>

C   Talk her editor into letting her go on the trip

D   Study maps of the United States

Common Core Standard RL.4.1

☐ **After Nellie Bly arrived in England she ____**

A   checked into a hotel

B   sent a story back home

C   set sail from Hoboken Pier

D   traveled from New York

Common Core Standard RI.4.3

☐ **When did Nellie Bly buy a monkey?**

A   Before she arrived in France

B   When she left Hoboken Pier

C   When the ship docked in San Francisco

D   Before she arrived in Japan

Common Core Standard RI.4.1

☐ **How did Nellie Bly travel across the United States?**

A   Walking

B   Airplane

C   Ship

D   Train

Common Core Standard RI.4.1

☐ **How many fewer days did it take Nellie Bly to travel around the world than it took Jules Verne?**

A   Ten days

B   Eight days

C   Six days

D   Seventy-two days

Common Core Standard RI.4.1

☐ **What was Nellie Bly's job at the newspaper?**

A   Reporter

B   Editor

C   Salesperson

D   Secretary

Name _____

Common Core Standard RI.4.1

☐ **Nellie Bly's journey began in _____**

A   France

B   England

C   New York

D   China

Common Core Standard RI.4.1

☐ **Nellie Bly rode a donkey in _____**

A   England

B   Port Said

C   Japan

D   China

Common Core Standard RI.4.1

☐ **What was the last country Nellie Bly visited before she returned to the United States?**

A   China

B   Suez Canal

C   San Francisco

D   Japan

Common Core Standard RI.4.7

☐ **According to the map, where did Nellie Bly's journey begin?**

A   Jersey City

B   San Francisco

C   Hong Kong

D   Singapore

Common Core Standard RI.4.7

☐ **According to the map, what was the fifth place Nellie Bly visited?**

A   London

B   Amiens

C   Brindisi

D   Port Said

Common Core Standard RI.4.7

☐ **What continent is Hong Kong located in?**

A   China

B   Africa

C   Asia

D   North America

Common Core Standard RI.4.2

☐ **What is the main idea of this passage?**

A Nellie Bly traveled around the world in less than eighty days.

B Nellie Bly bought a pet monkey and brought it back to the United States.

C Nellie Bly could not be talked out of making the long journey.

D Nellie Bly wanted to beat the author of the book <u>Around the World in Eighty Days</u>.

Common Core Standard RI.4.2, Common Core Standard RL.4.7

☐ **What is the main idea of the map found at the bottom of the page?**

A The oceans Nellie Bly crossed

B The hardships of Nellie Bly's journey

C Places Nellie Bly visited on her journey

D Where Nellie Bly started her journey

Common Core Standard RI.4.2

☐ **What is the main idea of the first paragraph of the passage?**

A Nellie Bly wanted to write stories about going around the world in less than eighty days.

B Everyone had read a new book.

C Nellie Bly's real name was Elizabeth Cochrane.

D Nellie Bly's editor was John Cockerill.

Name _____

Common Core Standard RI.4.2

☐   **What is the fourth paragraph mostly about?**

A   When Nellie Bly set sail from San Francisco, she was ready for her journey around the world.

B   When Nellie Bly left Hoboken Pier on her trip around the world, she carried only one small piece of luggage.

C   Nellie Bly had a 16 × 7 inch piece of luggage for her trip around the world.

D   Nellie Bly left from New York on her trip around the world.

Common Core Standard RI.4.2

☐   **What is this passage mostly about?**

A   Nellie Bly was a famous lady reporter who went on an exciting journey.

B   Nellie Bly traveled through many cities on her journey around the world.

C   Nellie Bly, a newspaper reporter, set out on a journey around the world to beat the record of 80 days.

D   While traveling around the world, Nellie Bly met many fascinating people and visited exciting places.

Common Core Standard RI.4.2

☐   **What is the last paragraph of the passage mostly about?**

A   When Nellie Bly arrived back in New York from her trip around the world, she was a famous lady who had beaten the record of 80 days.

B   Nellie Bly traveled 25,000 miles on her trip around the world.

C   Nellie Bly made the trip around the world in 72 days to beat the record of 80 days.

D   After Nellie Bly broke the record of 80 days, she came back to New York to celebrate.

Common Core Standard RI.4.5

☐ What caused a delay on Nellie Bly's journey around the world?

A   Nellie Bly bought a monkey in China.

B   Nellie Bly had to travel across mountains, rivers, and deserts.

C   After Nellie Bly's ship left Japan, they were in a terrible storm.

D   When Nellie Bly rode the donkey, the traveling was very slow.

Common Core Standard RI.4.5

☐ Readers in America looked at maps while Nellie Bly was on her journey because they _____

A   wanted to follow her route

B   were afraid she would get lost

C   read the newspaper

D   liked Nellie Bly

Common Core Standard RI.4.5

☐ Nellie Bly's editor believed she could probably break the record of 80 days because _____

A   she was 22 years old

B   when she made up her mind to do something, she was determined

C   she would leave from New York and return to San Francisco

D   she knew Jules Verne

Name _____

Common Core Standard RL.4.3

☐   **Which of the following is most likely to happen in the future?**

    A   Nellie Bly will go around the world again.

    B   Nellie Bly's editor will allow her to do another unusual assignment.

    C   Nellie Bly will become the editor of the newspaper.

    D   Jules Verne will try to beat Nellie Bly's record.

Common Core Standard RL.4.3

☐   **Why did Nellie Bly probably buy the monkey on the trip?**

    A   She had another pet monkey at home.

    B   She had read many articles about monkeys.

    C   She wanted a pet from her trip to keep her company.

    D   She liked monkeys and would not be able to buy one in the United States.

Common Core Standard RL.4.3

☐   **If the readers back in America had not liked Nellie Bly's stories, she would probably have _____**

    A   lost the race

    B   come home early

    C   not been famous

    D   written a different story

Common Core Standard RI.4.6

[ ] **How were Jules Verne and Nellie Bly alike?**

A   They were newspaper reporters.

B   They lived in New York City.

C   They liked adventures.

D   They bought a monkey in China.

Common Core Standard RI.4.6

[ ] **How were Jules Verne and Nellie Bly's stories of their journeys different?**

A   Jules Verne wrote about traveling on airplanes, and Nellie Bly wrote about traveling on ships.

B   Jules Verne wrote a book about his journey, and Nellie Bly wrote newspaper stories.

C   Nellie Bly wrote about mountains, rivers, temples, and camels, and Jules Verne wrote about deserts, elephants, and jewels.

D   Nellie Bly and Jules Verne wrote the same kind of stories.

Common Core Standard RI.4.3

[ ] **Why did people come to see Nellie Bly as she traveled across the country?**

A   They thought she was very pretty.

B   She had beaten Jules Verne's record of 80 days.

C   Her editor had asked people to cheer her on.

D   Nellie Bly had become a famous woman reporter.

Common Core Standard RL.4.3

☐   The reader can tell that Nellie Bly _____

A   was not afraid to try something new

B   wrote funny stories

C   was glad to get home

D   wanted to be editor of *The World*

Common Core Standard RL.4.3

☐   The reader can tell that no one had ever _____

A   written stories about their journey

B   traveled around the world in more than 80 days

C   traveled around the world

D   traveled around the world in less than 80 days

Common Core Standard RL.4.3

☐   The reader can tell that if Nellie Bly's editor had not allowed her to make the journey, she would have _____

A   cried

B   quit her job at *The World*

C   written stories about prisons

D   decided to make the trip later

Common Core Standard RL.4.3

☐ **Which of these words best describes how Nellie Bly probably felt about her journey?**

A   **Thrilled**

B   **Concerned**

C   **Worried**

D   **Tired**

Common Core Standard RL.4.3

☐ **How did the people in America probably feel when they saw Nellie Bly?**

A   **Nervous**

B   **Disappointed**

C   **Proud**

D   **Wise**

Common Core Standard RL.4.3

☐ **Information in this passage suggests that Nellie Bly was _____**

A   **used to making long journeys**

B   **known as a world traveler**

C   **used to making a lot of mistakes**

D   **used to taking risks**

Common Core Standard RL.4.2

☐ In this story, Nellie Bly's biggest problem was _____

A   bringing a monkey into the United States

B   sending the stories back to the newspaper

C   packing her clothes in the small bag

D   making the trip in less than 80 days

Common Core Standard RL.4.3

☐ How would the story have changed if Nellie Bly had not beaten Jules Verne's record?

A   The people in America would not have been proud of her.

B   She would not have been the most famous woman on earth.

C   Her editor would not have printed her stories.

D   She would have quit her job as a newspaper reporter.

Common Core Standard RL.4.7

☐ Where did Nellie Bly's journey begin and end?

A   New York

B   San Francisco

C   Hoboken Pier

D   England

Name _____

Common Core Standard RI.4.3

☐   **When did Nellie Bly travel across the United States?**

A   At the beginning of her journey

B   In the middle of her journey

C   Before she went to London

D   At the end of her journey

Common Core Standard RI.4.1, Common Core Standard RL.4.7

☐   **What ocean did Nellie Bly cross when she left Hong Kong?**

A   Pacific Ocean

B   Atlantic Ocean

C   Gulf of Mexico

D   Caribbean Ocean

Common Core Standard RL.4.7

☐   **According to the map, which continent did Nellie Bly not visit?**

A   North America

B   Africa

C   South America

D   Asia

Common Core Standard RL.4.7

☐ **Jersey City is located near ____**

    A   **San Francisco**

    B   **New York City**

    C   **London**

    D   **England**

Common Core Standard RI.4.8

☐ **The route Nellie Bly chose to go around the world was probably ____**

    A   **the least expensive way to travel**

    B   **the same route Jules Verne had taken**

    C   **the fastest way to travel**

    D   **the easiest way to travel**

Common Core Standard RI.4.1

☐ **Where is the city of London located?**

    A   **China**

    B   **Africa**

    C   **Japan**

    D   **England**

Name _____

Common Core Standard RI.4.1, Common Core Standard RL 4.1

☐ **Which of these is a FACT in this passage?**

A Nellie Bly was only twenty-five years old when she made her famous journey.

B The editor had learned that Nellie Bly was determined.

C Nellie Bly was the most famous woman on earth.

D Nellie Bly crossed the Atlantic Ocean on her way to London.

Common Core Standard RI.4.1, Common Core Standard RL.4.1

☐ **Which of these is an OPINION in this passage?**

A Nellie Bly carried only one piece of luggage on her journey.

B In China, Nellie Bly bought a monkey.

C Everyone was talking about a new book, *Around the World in Eighty Days*.

D A storm occurred while Nellie Bly was sailing to San Francisco.

Common Core Standard RI.4.1, Common Core Standard RL.4.1

☐ **Which of these is a FACT in this passage?**

A Everyone cheered when Nellie Bly stepped off the ship in San Francisco.

B Nellie Bly's real name was Elizabeth Cochrane.

C Nellie Bly had a unique idea.

D Nellie Bly traveled on a ship across France.

Common Core Standard RL.4.2

☐ This passage was probably written to _____

A   describe how to make a long journey

B   tell about a newspaper editor

C   tell about a famous person

D   give an opinion about travel

Common Core Standard RL.4.2

☐ The author probably wrote this passage so that _____

A   Nellie Bly would be famous

B   people could learn about the adventures of Nellie Bly

C   someone could try to beat Nellie Bly's record

D   he would get paid a lot of money

Common Core Standard RL.4.2

☐ This passage could be used to _____

A   teach people how to pack for a long trip

B   tell about other countries

C   help solve a problem

D   teach about courageous women

Common Core Standard RI.4.8, Common Core Standard RI.4.6

☐   The author of this passage probably believes that ____

A   Nellie Bly was a very brave young woman

B   Nellie Bly was a fake

C   Nellie Bly's editor should not have allowed her to make the trip

D   Jules Verne should have won the race

Common Core Standard RI.4.6, Common Core Standard RI.4.8

☐   The author of this passage probably thinks that ____

A   Nellie Bly should not have made the trip

B   more women should make long journeys

C   Nellie Bly was a good newspaper reporter

D   Nellie Bly's stories were dull

Common Core Standard RI.4.6, Common Core Standard RI.4.8

☐   The author of this passage probably wants the readers to ____

A   read another story about Nellie Bly

B   understand how unusual it was for a woman to make a long journey alone in 1888

C   know that Jules Verne had written a book

D   buy more of his stories

Sophie and the Magic Watering Can

Little Sophie, how she loved the garden
Watering all the pretty flowers.
One hot day she took a watering can
Not knowing it had magical <u>powers</u>.

As she sprinkled the water upon the blooms
She felt something strange was to come.
For all the flowers started moving, you see,
Shimmying in the summer sun.

Little Sophie gasped in disbelief
For the flowers were dancing it seemed.
"But flowers don't dance. That's silly!" she laughed.
"Such curious things I've never dreamed!"

But surely enough they bounced away
Swinging and bobbing quite lively.
And things got stranger as Sophie gasped,
"Are these faces I see before me?"

And so it was, each one of the blossoms
Had a tiny beaming face.
They chuckled and giggled with so much joy
As the garden became a magical place.

Sophie shrieked with much excitement
And clapped her little hands in <u>delight</u>.
"Oh flowers!" she beamed. "This is so much fun!
Let us dance long into the night!"

As Sophie and the flowers all frolicked away
Septimus, the cat, slinked by.
"Oh, Sep, join in. Shake your stripes!" laughed Sophie.
"Do cats dance too? Give it a try."

"No, cats cannot dance," said Sep, looking afraid.
"And flowers only do in the wind and rain.
And as this fine day is as <u>still</u> as can be
I fear for the <u>sanity</u> of my moggy brain!"

As poor Sep scuttled away clearly shaken
The dancing got into full swing.
But then, all of a sudden, the sky, it darkened
And down came the rain soaking everything.
But Sophie didn't care about the rain,
She loved the summer showers.

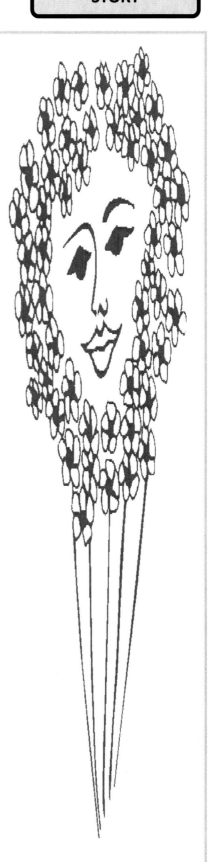

As the drops grew ever more steady
It quickly stilled the flowers.

It seemed this fantastical mystical spell
Did not agree with the rain.
For the flowers stopped dancing and all their wee faces
Had at once disappeared again.

"Goodbye, my little friends," sighed Sophie
As she glanced down at the ground.
But she still had the <u>magical</u> watering can
And tomorrow they would dance once more all around.

What Happens to Christmas?

A special treat comes every year
On the 25th of December,
Christmas comes to every town
But here is something to remember.

It only visits once a year
What happens when it's gone?
So where does Christmas go?
Where does it hide all year long?

Maybe it goes with Thanksgiving Day
On holiday to rest,
Or maybe a beach that no one knows
To swim and sun in the West.

Maybe it naps in a shed
In spring's garden, out of view,
On Christmas Eve, Easter may creep in
And wake it with a "Boo!"

Maybe it is among us
All year round, in <u>disguise</u>,
With its winter overcoat and
Dark glasses on its eyes.

Next time I will ask Christmas
If it can stay all year,
For it can stay at my house and
Together we shall eat cookies and drink milk here.

Common Core Standard RI.4.4

☐ In "Sophie and the Magical Watering Can," the word <u>sanity</u> means _____

A   cleanliness

B   protection

C   good sense

D   crazy

Common Core Standard RI.4.4

☐ In "Sophie and the Magical Watering Can," the word <u>magical</u> means _____

A   suspicious

B   supernatural

C   expensive

D   owned by a wizard

Common Core Standard RI.4.4

☐ In "What Happens to Christmas?", the word <u>disguise</u> means _____

A   unable to recognize

B   sneaky

C   hiding

D   famous

Common Core Standard RL.4.4

☐   Read the meanings below for the word <u>power</u>.

Which meaning best fits the way <u>powers</u> is used in "Sophie and the Magic Watering Can?"

A   Meaning 3

B   Meaning 2

C   Meaning 4

D   Meaning 1

> power (´swing) *noun*
> 1. A nation that has influence among other nations.   2. The ability to act or to do.   3. Force or energy used to do work.   4. Physical strength.

Common Core Standard RL.4.4

☐   Read the meanings below for the word <u>delight</u>.

Which meaning best fits the way <u>delight</u> is used in "Sophie and the Magic Watering Can?"

A   Meaning 1

B   Meaning 2

C   Meaning 4

D   Meaning 3

> delight (di-´līt) *noun*
> 1. Great pleasure or satisfaction; joy.
> 2. Something that gives great pleasure.
> *verb*
> 3. To take great pleasure.
> 4. To give joy or satisfaction to.

Common Core Standard RL.4.4

☐   Read the meanings below for the word <u>still</u>.

Which meaning best fits the way <u>still</u> is used in "Sophie and the Magic Watering Can?"

A   Meaning 3

B   Meaning 2

C   Meaning 4

D   Meaning 1

> still (´stil) *noun*
> 1. Quiet, silence.
> *verb*
> 2. To make or become quiet.
> *adverb*
> 3. Without motion.
> 4. To grind into flour or powder.

Name _____

Common Core Standard RI.4.2

☐   Where does "Sophie and the Magic Watering Can" take place?

A   At her house

B   Near a pond

C   In the park

D   In her garden

Common Core Standard RI.4.3, Common Core Standard RL.4.3

☐   Septimus, the cat, does not believe the flowers are dancing because _____

A   he has never seen them dancing

B   cats cannot dance

C   he probably does not believe in magic

D   he thinks he is going crazy

Common Core Standard RL.4.7

☐   Look at the diagram about Sophie and Septimus. Which of the following goes in the blank?

Sophie

*Saw faces on the
  flowers
*Believed in the magic
  watering can

*In the garden

Septimus

*Could not dance
*_____

A   Became afraid and upset   C   Danced with the flowers

B   Laughed and giggled   D   Disappeared when it rained

Common Core Standard RI.4.5

☐ How does the author of "What Happens to Christmas?" solve the problem for Christmas?

A He wants Christmas to eat cookies and drink milk.

B He wants Christmas to stay with him.

C He wants Christmas to come one day a year.

D He wants Christmas to go away.

Common Core Standard RI.4.3, Common Core Standard RL.4.3

☐ Look at this diagram of information from "Sophie and the Magic Watering Can." Which idea belongs in the empty box?

Sophie		
Danced with the flowers	Liked summer showers	

A Feared for her sanity   C Felt something magical was about to happen

B Did not like to dance   D Did not believe in magic

Common Core Standard RI.4.1

☐ Where will Sophie go tomorrow?

A To the garden

B To see Septimus

C To find the magic

D To her house

Common Core Standard RL.4.7

☐ **Look at the web about the poem. Which of these belongs in the empty circle?**

A Something to remember

B Maybe it goes on holiday

C Maybe it stays at home

D Stays all year

Maybe it naps in a shed

What Happens to Christmas

Maybe it swims and suns

Common Core Standard RI.4.1, Common Core Standard RL.4.1

☐ **What is the total amount of time that Christmas is gone?**

A 25th of December

B 55 weeks

C 12 months

D 360 days

Common Core Standard RL.4.2

☐ **Explain in your own words why Septimus became upset when Sophie wanted him to dance with the flowers.**

_____

_____

_____

_____

_____

Common Core Standard RL.4.3, Common Core Standard RL.4.8

☐ **Why did the flowers begin to dance?**

A   Sophie began to dance.

B   They were given magic water.

C   It was beginning to rain.

D   All of the flowers started to move.

Common Core Standard RL.4.3

☐ **What will probably happen if Sophie uses the watering can to water the shrubs?**

A   The shrubs will become Sophie's new friends.

B   The shrubs will dance with Septimus.

C   The shrubs will begin to grow.

D   The shrubs will be given magical powers.

Common Core Standard RL.4.3, Common Core Standard RI.4.8

☐ **Why did the flowers stop dancing?**

A   The flowers were tired.

B   The flowers were not thirsty.

C   The spell was broken by the rain.

D   Sophie went into her house.

Common Core Standard RI.4.5, Common Core Standard RL.4.2

☐   **Why did Easter wake Christmas on Christmas Eve?**

_____

_____

_____

_____

_____

_____

Common Core Standard RI.4.1, Common Core Standard RL.4.1

☐   **Which line from "Sophie and the Magic Watering Can" could not happen?**

A   *Little Sophie gasped in disbelief*

B   *As she sprinkled the water upon the blooms*

C   *They chuckled and giggled with so much joy*

D   *Sophie shrieked with much excitement*

Common Core Standard RI.4.8

☐   **Which of the following could be reason Sophie loved the summer showers?**

A   The showers cooled the air on hot days.

B   The showers flooded the rivers.

C   The showers were fun to watch.

D   The flowers did not want to dance in the rain.

Name _____

Common Core Standard RL.4.5

☐ How can you tell "What Happens to Christmas?" is a poem?

A   It does not have sentences.

B   It is a fictitious story with imaginary characters.

C   It does not have punctuation at the end of each line.

D   It has 6 paragraphs.

Common Core Standard RL.4.2, Common Core Standard RL.4.5

☐ Explain in your own words why you believe "Sophie and the Magic Watering Can" could or could not happen.

_____

_____

_____

_____

_____

_____

Common Core Standard RI.4.2, Common Core Standard RL.4.2

☐ "Sophie and the Magic Watering Can" is a poem that _____

A   tells a story about a cat

B   tells a make-believe story

C   teaches a lesson

D   does not make sense

Common Core Standard RI.4.1

☐ From information in "What Happen to Christmas?" which statement would be reasonable?

A   Thanksgiving Day is not an important holiday.

B   A holiday happens once every year.

C   Easter wakes Christmas each year.

D   There are 4 holidays each year.

Common Core Standard RL.4.2

☐ The theme of "Sophie and the Magic Watering Can" is mostly about _____

A   a day when the flowers danced with Sophie

B   a rainy day

C   a cat that could not dance

D   Sophie's garden

Common Core Standard RL.4.2, Common Core Standard RL.4.5

☐ Referring to the third verse, explain in your own words where you believe Christmas goes each year.

_____

_____

_____

_____

_____

_____

Common Core Standard RI.4.2

☐   "What Happens to Christmas?" is mostly about ____

   A   the places Christmas might go each year

   B   all of the holidays that occur in one year

   C   the author's favorite holiday

   D   when holidays occur

Common Core Standard RL.4.3

☐   How did Septimus feel when Sophie invited him to join in the dancing?

   A   Guilty

   B   Silly

   C   Grumpy

   D   Disturbed

Common Core Standard RL.4.7

☐   Which of the following would be a good title for "What Happens to Christmas?"

   A   Holidays during December

   B   Christmas is Hiding

   C   Christmas Comes Once a Year

   D   My Favorite Holiday

Name _____

Common Core Standard RI.4.8

☐ **Why do you think the author wrote "What Happens to Christmas?"**

_____

_____

_____

_____

_____

_____

Common Core Standard RI.4.8

☐ **The author of "Sophie and the Magic Watering Can" probably included the verses about Septimus, the cat, ____**

A   so the poem would have an animal in it

B   to show that only Sophie experienced the magic

C   because the author does not like cats

D   to include something evil in the poem

Common Core Standard RI.4.9, Common Core Standard RL.4.9

☐ **"Sophie and the Magic Watering Can" and "What Happens to Christmas?" are ____**

A   boring

B   scary

C   fun to read

D   too long

Name _____

Common Core Standard RI.4.3

☐ Tell in your own words why you think Sophie will use the magical watering can again.

_____

_____

_____

_____

_____

_____

Common Core Standard RI.4.3

☐ What happened after Septimus walked away?

A   Sophie asked him to shake his stripes.

B   Sophie saw faces on the flowers.

C   The flowers began to dance more enthusiastically.

D   The watering can had magical powers.

Common Core Standard RL.4.3

☐ What did Septimus mean when he said he had a "moggy brain?"

A   He was not very smart.

B   He was confused.

C   He was very forgetful.

D   He thought Sophie was acting strangely.

Common Core Standard RL.4.5

☐ **Both texts are written in the same form that rhymes. This means both texts are** ___

    A   easy to read

    B   written from a first-person

    C   poems

    D   dramas with different characters

Common Core Standard RL.4.6

☐ **What point of view does the author of the poems describe the events?**

    A   "Sophie and the Magic Watering Can" is written as a third person, while "What Happens to Christmas?" is written as a first person.

    B   Both poems are written as a third person.

    C   Both poems are written as a first person.

    D   "What Happens to Christmas?" is written as a third person, while "Sophie and the Magic Watering Can" is written as a first person.

Common Core Standard RL.4.5

☐ **Choose what is right.**
The author separates the sequence of events in the following way:

    A   "Sophie and the Magic Watering Can" has 12 verses, and "What Happens to Christmas?" has 6 verses.

    B   Each poem has 18 verses.

    C   Each verse is a new story.

    D   The author started new event with a new paragraph.

The Life of a Whale

1   Humans have always been fascinated by whales. Whether it is their size, their appearance, or the mysterious stories about whales, they remain an interesting topic to study among the young and old.

Are whales mammals?

2   Mammals are animals that are born alive and feed on their mother's milk. They breathe air and are warm-blooded, keeping the same body temperature regardless of how cold or warm their surroundings. All mammals have hair, even if it is only a few bristles like the whale.

3   Whales belong to a group of sea-dwelling mammals that includes dolphins and porpoises. These animals are called cetaceans (sih-TAY-shuns). Cetaceans have the shape of fish and live in the water, but they are mammals.

How do whales care for their young?

4   Whales usually have only one baby at a time. Sometimes twins are born, but this is rare. A baby whale is called a calf. Female whales, known as cows, carry their unborn young for about 18 months. Most cows give birth every two to five years.

5   Calves drink mothers' milk, just like other mammals. The calf swallows a huge stream of milk that the cow squirts into the throat of the calf. The calf surfaces for a quick breath of air. They can gain as much as 200 pounds a day.

How do whales breathe?

6   Whales breathe through nostrils called blowholes. The blowholes are on the top of the head. The blowholes let whales breathe even when most of their body is under the water. When whales take a deep dive, they fill their lungs with air and hold their breath. Sooner or later, they must come to the surface for a breath of fresh air. But first, the whale blasts out the stale air, called the blow, at a speed of about 300 miles per hour.

7   Sometimes a whale blows just below the surface of the water. The blow looks like a puffy cloud. The air the whale breathes out is warm and moist. When it hits the colder outside air, it forms a cloud of tiny drops of water. The blow sprays seawater with the escaping air. A single blow can be as high as a three-story building.

How long can whales stay underwater?

8   Whales can hold their breath longer than humans. Even the best human diver can stay underwater only a few minutes without coming up for air. The whale can remain underwater from 20 minutes to 2 hours.

9   Whale blood holds more oxygen than human blood. After taking several deep breaths before it dives, the whale draws on this stored-up supply of oxygen. Humans only fill about one-fourth of their lungs with air, while whales fill almost all of their lungs. When the air is gone, the whale returns to the surface of the water and the process begins again.

10   Whales can drown if water enters their blowholes. This happens when whales get sick, hurt, or tangled up in nets or lines under the sea. If a whale is disabled and cannot swim to the surface to breathe, it will drown.

Can whales see and hear?

11   The ears of a whale are two tiny holes in the skin on its head. The rest of the ear is inside its head just like human ears. Even though these openings are very small, they give whales the most remarkable hearing. Whales can hear sounds much higher and lower than humans. Some whales can hear underwater sounds from as far away as 1,000 miles.

12   Whales have fairly good <u>vision</u>, but most cannot see very far under the water. Ocean waters are dark and <u>murky</u>, so often it is unrealistic to believe they can see more than a few feet ahead. Most use sound, not sight, to <u>detect</u> objects underwater. For example, when sound hits an object it <u>echoes</u> back. If the echo comes back quickly, the whale knows the object is close. If it takes longer, the object is farther away.

Where do whales live?

13   Whales live in all of the oceans of the world. Some stay in the icy cold waters near the North and South Poles all year long. Others never leave the warm tropical seas. However, some <u>migrate</u> twice a year, in the spring and fall, to find food. These <u>journeys</u> are some of the longest of any animal. They may cover thousands of miles and take a few months.

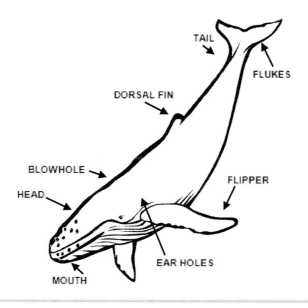

Common Core Standard RI.4.4

☐   In this passage, the word <u>appearance</u> means _____

   A   to be seen

   B   looks like

   C   brightness

   D   where live

Common Core Standard RI.4.4

☐   In this passage, the word <u>surroundings</u> means _____

   A   to circle

   B   ocean

   C   environment

   D   way to travel

Common Core Standard RI.4.4, Common Core Standard RL.4.4

☐   In this passage, the word <u>bristles</u> means _____

   A   hair brush

   B   soft hair

   C   angry

   D   stiff and rough hair

Common Core Standard RL.4.4

☐ In this passage, the word <u>stream</u> means _____

A   smooth movement of liquid

B   small body of water

C   long pieces of paper

D   traveling a short distance

Common Core Standard RI.4.4

☐ In this passage, the word <u>nostrils</u> means _____

A   the face

B   openings

C   large heads

D   ears

Common Core Standard RL.4.4

☐ In this passage, the word <u>stale</u> means _____

A   wet

B   dirty

C   old

D   new

Common Core Standard RL.4.4

☐　　In this passage, the word <u>puffy</u> means _____

　　A　　dark

　　B　　very wet

　　C　　bright

　　D　　full of air

Common Core Standard RL.4.4

☐　　In this passage, the word <u>draws</u> means _____

　　A　　work of art

　　B　　to sketch

　　C　　uses

　　D　　paints

Common Core Standard RL.4.4

☐　　In this passage, the word <u>process</u> means _____

　　A　　way of doing

　　B　　to make straight

　　C　　swimming

　　D　　breathing

Common Core Standard RI.4.4

☐   In this passage, the word <u>tangled</u> means _____

    A   noticed

    B   straight

    C   twisted

    D   colored

Common Core Standard RL.4.4

☐   In this passage, the word <u>vision</u> means _____

    A   swimming

    B   seeing

    C   hearing

    D   feeling

Common Core Standard RL.4.4

☐   In this passage, the word <u>detect</u> means _____

    A   locate

    B   see

    C   eat

    D   fight

Name _____

Common Core Standard RI.4.4

☐　　In this passage, the word <u>echoes</u> means _____

A　　is seen from far away

B　　bounces back

C　　yelling loudly

D　　easy to reach

Common Core Standard RL.4.4

☐　　In this passage, the word <u>migrate</u> means _____

A　　move from place to place

B　　live far away

C　　go on vacation

D　　escape from enemies

Common Core Standard RL.4.4

☐　　In this passage, the word <u>journeys</u> means _____

A　　meals

B　　mammals

C　　tails

D　　trips

Common Core Standard RI.4.4

☐ **In this passage, the word <u>unborn</u> means ____**

A   too small

B   not born

C   egg

D   very large

Common Core Standard RL.4.4

☐ **In this passage, the word <u>disabled</u> means ____**

A   blind

B   old and sick

C   frightened

D   helpless

Common Core Standard RL.4.4

☐ **In this passage, the word <u>murky</u> means ____**

A   warm

B   clear

C   cloudy

D   cold

Common Core Standard RI.4.5

☐ **What does the whale do before it takes a breath of fresh air?**

    A   Swim on the bottom of the ocean

    B   Make a deep dive

    C   Blow out the old air in their lungs

    D   Travel 300 miles per hour

Common Core Standard RI.4.5

☐ **What must sound do before it echoes back?**

    A   Hit an object

    B   Make a loud noise

    C   Go under the water

    D   Move far away

Common Core Standard RI.4.5

☐ **What does the whale do after the air in their lungs is all gone?**

    A   Sink to the bottom of the ocean

    B   Return to the top of the water

    C   Drown

    D   Dive into the water

Common Core Standard RI.4.5

☐ **How are cetaceans different from fish?**

A Fish live in water.

B Cetaceans have the same shape as fish.

C Cetaceans are mammals.

D Fish are mammals.

Common Core Standard RI.4.3

☐ **Why do some whales migrate in the fall and spring?**

A To find food

B To give birth

C To move to warmer water

D To move to colder water

Common Core Standard RI.4.3

☐ **How long can a whale hold its breath?**

A 0 to 18 months

B 300 miles

C A few minutes

D Up to 2 hours

Common Core Standard RI.4.1

☐ Where are whales when they blow out the stale air?

A   At the bottom of the ocean

B   Below the surface of the water

C   On the beach

D   During a dive into the water

Common Core Standard RI.4.1

☐ In which oceans can whales be found?

A   Only in oceans with cold water

B   Only in oceans with warm water

C   Only in deep oceans

D   In all oceans

Common Core Standard RI.4.1

☐ When do mother whales give birth?

A   Every year

B   Every two to ten years

C   Every two to five years

D   Every five years

Common Core Standard RI.4.2

☐ **What is the main idea of this passage?**

A   The whale is a mammal that can live in warm and cold water.

B   Whales look like fish, but are mammals.

C   Whales breathe through nostrils in their head.

D   Whales are an interesting mammal.

Common Core Standard RI.4.2

☐ **What is the main idea of the section "Can Whales See and Hear?"**

A   Whales have better hearing than sight.

B   Whales hear through two tiny holes in their head.

C   Whales use echoes to see objects.

D   Most whales use sound to find objects under water.

Common Core Standard RI.4.2

☐ **What is the main idea of the section "How Long Can Whales Stay Underwater?"**

A   Whales use their blowholes to breathe.

B   When whales fill their lungs, they can stay underwater for long periods of time.

C   Whales will drown if they get tangled in nets.

D   Whales are better swimmers than humans.

Name _____

Common Core Standard RL.4.2

☐   **What is this passage mostly about?**

A   Whales are mammals who live in the oceans of the world, breathe through blowholes, can see and hear under water, and feed milk to their young.

B   The whale is a mammal that lives near the North and South Poles and breathes through a blowhole.

C   Dolphins, porpoises, and whales are mammals that feed mother's milk to their young.

D   After the whale blows at the top of the water, it will then dive to the bottom of the ocean and remain for up to 2 hours.

Common Core Standard RL.4.2

☐   **What is the section "How Do Whales Breathe?" mostly about?**

A   Whales blast out the stale air at a speed of about 300 miles per hour.

B   A single blow can be as high as a three-story building and contains seawater with the air.

C   Whales blow air through blowholes on the top of their head even when most of their body is under the water.

D   Blowholes spray seawater with air which forms a cloud.

Common Core Standard RL.4.2

☐   **What is the section "Where Do Whales Live?" mostly about?**

A   Whales live near the North and South Poles.

B   Whales live in all oceans and some even migrate.

C   Some whales migrate twice a year to find food.

D   Whales may migrate as many as 1000 miles a year.

Common Core Standard RL.4.1

[ ]   What can happen to a whale if it gets tangled in nets under the water?

A   The whale can get sick.

B   The whale will drown.

C   The whale will swim to the top of the water.

D   The whale will hold its breath.

Common Core Standard RL.4.1

[ ]   When whales dive deep into the water, they can hold their breath because they _____

A   have a blowhole

B   live in the ocean

C   are warm-blooded

D   fill their lungs with air

Common Core Standard RL.4.1

[ ]   Whales can hold their breath longer than humans because they _____

A   are mammals

B   have a blowhole

C   fill almost all of their lungs with air

D   breathe air

Common Core Standard RL.4.3

☐   **Why are whales able to live in cold and warm water?**

A   **They have blowholes that allow them to dive under the water.**

B   **They migrate thousands of miles each year.**

C   **They are warm-blooded keeping the same body temperature.**

D   **They are born alive.**

Common Core Standard RL.4.3

☐   **Why are whales not able to see very far in the water?**

A   **The water can be dark and cloudy.**

B   **They have small eyes.**

C   **Whales do not use their eyes for seeing.**

D   **The water is too cold.**

Common Core Standard RL.4.3

☐   **Whales, dolphins, and porpoises are mammals because they ____**

A   **live in the sea**

B   **are mysterious**

C   **are called calves**

D   **are born alive**

Name _____

Common Core Standard RL.4.1

☐   **According to the passage, whales use their hearing for ____**

     A   finding objects under the water

     B   swimming

     C   finding food

     D   blowing a puffy cloud

Common Core Standard RL.4.9

☐   **Whales and humans are alike because they can ____**

     A   gain 200 pounds a day

     B   live in cold and warm water

     C   hear underwater sounds 1000 miles away

     D   stay under the water

Common Core Standard RL.4.9

☐   **The ears of a whale are like a humans because they are ____**

     A   very large

     B   inside its head

     C   used to see

     D   able to hear very high sounds

Common Core Standard RL.4.7

[ ] **The reader can tell that the whale is a large mammal because it _____**

A   swims under the water

B   can gain up to 200 pounds a day

C   is born alive

D   drinks mother's milk

Common Core Standard RL.4.7

[ ] **The reader can tell that the blow is like a cloud in the sky because it _____**

A   is big

B   is made of seawater

C   has drops of water in it

D   is dark

Common Core Standard RL.4.7

[ ] **The reader can tell that a whale must come to the top of the water because it needs _____**

A   air

B   food

C   milk

D   its mother

Name _____

Common Core Standard RL.4.3

☐ **How do whales probably feel when they become tangled in nets in the water?**

A **Proud**

B **Pleased**

C **Anxious**

D **Calm**

Common Core Standard RL.4.3

☐ **How do people usually feel when they see a whale blow?**

A **Disappointed**

B **Amazed**

C **Sorry**

D **Wise**

Common Core Standard RL.4.3

☐ **According to the passage, how do mother whales probably feel about their calves?**

A **Caring**

B **Curious**

C **Selfish**

D **Lazy**

Common Core Standard RI.4.5, Common Core Standard RL.4.8

☐ **Information in the passage suggests that the nets and lines that can harm a whale are probably a result of _____**

    A   other mammals

    B   fishing boats

    C   hunters

    D   sight-seeing boats

Common Core Standard RI.4.5, Common Core Standard RI.4.8

☐ **People enjoy watching whales because they _____**

    A   live in the ocean

    B   migrate

    C   have good hearing

    D   are large and blow

Common Core Standard RI.4.5, Common Core Standard RI.4.8

☐ **Whales are able to live in cold and warm water because they _____**

    A   always keep the same body temperature

    B   eat other fish

    C   are excellent swimmers

    D   can hear sound from 1000 miles away

Common Core Standard RI.4.6, Common Core Standard RL.4.1

☐   **Which of these is a FACT in this passage?**

    A   The ears of the whale are tiny, but they have can hear sounds as far away as 1000 miles.

    B   Whales are an interesting topic to study among the old and the young.

    C   Humans have always been fascinated by whales.

    D   The best human diver can stay underwater for a few minutes.

Common Core Standard RI.4.6, Common Core Standard RL.4.1

☐   **Which of these is an OPINION in this passage?**

    A   Whales live in all of the oceans of the world.

    B   A single blow can be as high as a three-story building.

    C   Whales can drown if water enters their blowholes.

    D   There have been many mysterious stories written about the whale.

Common Core Standard RI.4.6, Common Core Standard RL.4.1

☐   **Which of these is a FACT in this passage?**

    A   The blow of the whale looks like a puffy cloud.

    B   Whale babies depend on their mothers for protection from enemies.

    C   Whales must return to the surface of the water to fill their lungs with fresh air.

    D   Whales do not belong to the cetaceans group of mammals.

Common Core Standard RL.4.9

☐ This passage was probably written to _____

A   make people afraid of whales

B   give an opinion about whales

C   solve the problem of whales in the oceans

D   tell about the life of a whale

Common Core Standard RL.4.9

☐ The author probably wrote this passage to _____

A   show how the whale is like other mammals

B   help the whale become endangered

C   make fishermen keep their lines away from whales

D   show how dangerous the whale is

Common Core Standard RL.4.9

☐ This passage was probably written to _____

A   encourage people to protect whales

B   frighten the reader

C   tell about an interesting mammal

D   make the reader laugh

Common Core Standard RL.4.6

☐   **The author of this passage probably _____**

    A   believes whales are very interesting

    B   thinks people dislike whales

    C   thinks whales should be on the endangered list

    D   has whales for pets

Common Core Standard RL.4.6

☐   **The reader can tell that the author of this passage _____**

    A   dislikes whales

    B   thinks whales are useless

    C   knows a lot about whales

    D   wants readers to be concerned about whales

Common Core Standard RL.4.6

☐   **The author of this passage probably believes that whales _____**

    A   are beautiful

    B   are fascinating

    C   are not very smart

    D   live too long

Name _____

Wonders of the Food World

1   Have you ever eaten blue margarine or purple ketchup? Believe it or not, some people have. In the past ten years the makers of these strange foods have found an <u>audience</u> for these products, but some of the classics that have survived the sands of time are still the favorites of young and old eaters. Although many things have changed in our country over the years, such as fashions, music, presidents, and pro football teams, some foods have found the secret of remaining popular.

2   Among the successful seniors celebrating anniversaries in the 21st century were Oreo, which has been around for over 100 years, and Kool-Aid, which is 86 years old. Karo syrup and Barnum's Animal Crackers also observed their 111th birthdays. Krispy Kreme doughnuts are 75 years old, and Weber barbecue grills celebrated their 61st anniversary. These names are so familiar you probably have friends, parents, and grandparents who remember these products.

3   Have you ever walked animal crackers across a table? Have you ever pretended to be the Kool-Aid Man? Did your grandfather own a Weber grill? No matter their age, probably everyone has taken an Oreo cookie apart and eaten the filling first.

4   What keeps these traditions alive in our fast-paced, ever changing world? If you are going to search for the deep answer to this question, it would be better to do it over a plate of Oreos and a glass of milk for dunking your cookie. The more cookies you eat, the more ideas you will come up with!

5   The easy answer to that question is they are all instant gratification. They taste good and appeal to many ages and cultures. They are <u>affordable</u>, but high in quality and have widespread availability.

6   It is true that some of these products have changed significantly to reflect the times. Weber now has a mega gas grill system, Oreos have mint and peanut butter flavored fillings, and Kool-Aid has a no-sugar version. However, the companies have not <u>discarded</u> the old originals in favor of the new versions. Therein lies the nostalgia factor of passing favorite old tastes from one generation to another. It is possible that Oreos have been eaten by as many as six generations in a single family. Favorite foods may have the power to <u>link</u>, rather than drive apart, the generations in contrast to what clothing and music styles might do. This generational swap works both ways. It is not unusual for the younger set to introduce new versions of old favorites to their seniors.

7   No matter which of these generations you belong to, let us all join in and sing an anniversary song to these old favorites and pause for a few bites of food history.

Oreo, 101

Generically, they are known as chocolate sandwiches, but when they were born in New York in 1912, they were referred to as biscuits. This new cookie was baked by Nabisco, the National Biscuit Company.

Why were they called Oreos? It is hard to say. There are many guesses, but no official answer. Nevertheless, the black-and-white snack has been America's most popular cookie since its beginning, resulting in more than 450 billion consumed to date.

Kool-Aid, 86

When Kool-Aid was invented in Nebraska in 1927, it was spelled Kool-Ade. The sweet drink came in six flavors. As time passed, "Ade" became "Aid", and now 52 flavors have been created. Some unique flavors are Great Bluedini, Rock-a-Dile Red, and Pink Swimingo.

Gallon for gallon, Kool-Aid is the number one beverage consumed by children in the United States. During the summer, 26 gallons are gulped every second. One reason for its popularity is the cost, less than a nickel per glass. Kool-Aid has gone beyond the pitcher to plastic bottles, pouch drinks, and freezer pops.

Now do not forget the Kool-Aid Man, a character who gave the drink its identity. He made his wall-crashing entrances in 1975 shouting "Oh, yeah!" He was such a cool guy that he later was shown involved in sports and guitar jamming sessions. His popularity made him important enough to earn celebrity footprints at Mann's Chinese Theater in Hollywood, California.

Barnum's Animal Crackers, 111

Let's get the record straight. These are not really crackers. They are cookies, and they were not born in the USA. They were imported from England in the late 1800s.

The trademark theme of the colorful circus cage with the string handle was introduced in 1902. The boxes were given a string handle so they could be hung on a Christmas tree. The crackers became so popular they were sold year-round, not just during the Christmas holidays. Today, 300,000 animals are baked per hour, and in one year, 8,000 miles of string is attached to the little boxes.

Because the cookies are not overly sweet, they are one of the first cookies that parents give their small children. However, adults like to munch them also.

There currently are 18 circus animals in each box. As the result of a public poll, a koala bear was added in September, 2002, in honor of the 100 year anniversary.

Karo Syrup, 111

Before Karo light and dark corn syrups came into being in 1902, housewives had to take their syrup jugs to a store to be filled from barrels by the grocer.

However, Karo changed all that by putting the syrup into containers that looked like paint cans. Karo was first made by the Corn Products Refining Company of New York and Chicago.

The Karo name is believed to have been in honor of Caroline, the wife of the company's expert syrup creator. Another theory says it came from Kairomel, an earlier syrup trademark.

The company quickly published cookbooks using the products. In 1930, according to Karo's history, the wife of a corporate sales executive mixed the corn syrup with sugar, eggs, vanilla, and pecans for the now-classic pecan pie. This recipe continues to be called the Karo Pie in some areas.

Today, the product, which also includes a waffle syrup, is used as a topping for breakfast dishes and in pies, candies, glazes, sauces, beverages, and ice cream.

Krispy Kreme, 75

Vernon Rudolph obviously knew a good recipe when he saw one. In 1937, he bought a secret yeast-raised dough recipe from a French chef in New Orleans, Louisiana. He took it to Winston-Salem, North Carolina, and began making the hot sweets. He sold his product to local groceries, but then people began coming by his bakery asking for the hot treats. He cut a hole in the wall and sold directly to his customers. That was the beginning of Krispy Kreme doughnuts.

Today the light, shiny, frosted doughnuts have achieved nation wide appeal. Many people drive for miles seeking the 234 Krispy Kreme shops in the United States.

More than twenty varieties have been added to the original recipe. It has been estimated that the shops sell more than seven million doughnuts each day.

Weber, 61

It was not a metal <u>buoy</u> or a 55-gallon drum that George Stephen cut in half in 1952 trying to make a better grill than the open version. He wanted to keep out the rain and seal in the smoke, so he fashioned a dome-shaped lid. This idea was very daring at the time.

Mr. Stephen took a lot of teasing from his friends over his strange-looking contraption, but once they tasted the food cooked on the grill, they stopped laughing. People <u>willingly</u> spent $50 for the kettle grill when most grills sold for $7.

However, George had the last laugh. The grill sold so well he formed the barbecue division of Weber Brothers Metal Works in Mount Prospect, Illinois. In the late 1950s, he bought the company.

Common Core Standard RI.4.4

☐   In paragraph 6, the word <u>discarded</u> means _____

     A   lost

     B   thrown away

     C   sold

     D   tasted

Common Core Standard RI.4.4

☐   In paragraph 5, the word <u>affordable</u> means _____

     A   expensive

     B   tasty

     C   crunchy

     D   reasonably priced

Common Core Standard RI.4.4

☐   In the section "Weber, 61," the word <u>willingly</u> means _____

     A   cleverly

     B   very slow

     C   gladly

     D   not enthusiastic

Common Core Standard RL.4.4

☐   Read the meanings below for the word <u>audience</u>.

Which meaning best fits the way <u>audience</u> is used in paragraph 1?

A   Meaning 3

B   Meaning 2

C   Meaning 4

D   Meaning 1

> audience (´öd-ē-uns) *noun*
> 1. A group that listens or watches a performance. 2. A chance to talk with a person of very high rank. 3. Those of the general public who give attention to something said, done, or written. 4. A formal hearing or conference.

Common Core Standard RL.4.4

☐   Read the meanings below for the word <u>link</u>.

Which meaning best fits the way <u>link</u> is used in paragraph 6?

A   Meaning 3

B   Meaning 2

C   Meaning 4

D   Meaning 1

> link (´lingk) *verb*
> 1. To connect or become connected.
> *noun*
> 2. A single ring of a chain. 3. One of a series of things. 4. A bond or a tie.

Common Core Standard RL.4.4

☐   Read the meanings below for the word <u>buoy</u>.

Which meaning best fits the way <u>buoy</u> is used in the section "Weber, 61?"

A   Meaning 4

B   Meaning 2

C   Meaning 1

D   Meaning 3

> buoy (´bü-ē) *noun*
> 1. A floating object anchored in a body of water so as to mark a channel or to warn of danger. 2. A device made to keep a person afloat.
> *verb*
> 3. To keep afloat. 4. To cheer up.

Common Core Standard RI.4.5, Common Core Standard RL.4.1

☐ **The products discussed in the passage probably have not been changed because** ____

A   people recognize their names

B   they are not expensive

C   they sell as many of the originals now as were ever been sold in the past

D   the companies do not want to make new products

Common Core Standard RI.4.7, Common Core Standard RL.4.1

☐ **Look at the timeline of information from the passage. Which of these belongs in the empty box?**

Barnum's Animal Crackers imported from England.	Began selling Karo light and dark syrup.	Kool-Aid was invented.	Vernon Rudolph bought a recipe.	
1800s	1902	1927	1937	2002

A   Introduced koala bear   C   Sold 450 billion

B   Changed Kool-Aid's name   D   Bought company

Common Core Standard RI.4.5, Common Core Standard RL.4.1

☐ **The Oreo was probably called a biscuit when it was first introduced because** ____

A   it was baked by a biscuit company

B   it looked like a biscuit

C   no one knew what a cookie was

D   it tasted like a biscuit

Name _____

Comon Core Standard RI.4.7, Common Core Standard RL.4.1

☐ Look at this diagram of information from the article. Which idea belongs in the empty box?

```
                    Kool-Aid Man
        ┌───────────────┼───────────────┐
Earned celebrity     Involved in sports
footprints at        and guitar jamming
Mann's Chinese       sessions
Theater
```

A   Less than a nickel per glass   C   Is 68 years old

B   Created in 1975   D   Has 52 flavors

Common Core Standard RL.4.1

☐ Why did the company that makes Barnum Animal Crackers probably conduct a public poll to find which new animal should be added to the box of cookies?

A   They could not decide which animal needed to be added.

B   It brought attention to the cookies, and more people would buy the boxes of cookies to see the new animal.

C   People were not buying the boxes of cookies anymore.

D   They wanted to hear the children's ideas.

Common Core Standard RI.4.7, Common Core Standard RL.4.1

☐ Look at the diagram about Oreos and Barnum's Animal Crackers. Which information does *not* belong where it has been placed in the diagram?

Barnum's Animal Crackers
*Not born in USA
*Boxes have a string handle

*Cookies
*First cookie given to small children

Oreos
*Chocolate sandwiches
*450 billion consumed

A   Not born in USA   C   Cookie

B   450 billion consumed   D   First cookie given to small children

Common Core Standard RI.4.5, Common Core Standard RL.4.6

☐ **Parents probably give Barnum's Animal Crackers instead of Oreos as a first cookie to their small children because _____**

A   they are shaped like animals

B   they are cheaper to buy

C   they are not as large or as sweet as Oreos

D   Oreos are a chocolate cookie

Common Core Standard RI.4.5; RL.4.6

☐ **What might have been different in George Stephen's life if no one had liked his grill?**

A   He would have used his old grill to prepare foods.

B   He would have been angry with his friends because they laughed at him.

C   He would have invented a gas grill.

D   He would not have bought the company he worked for.

Common Core Standard RI.4.5, Common Core Standard RL.4.6

☐ **Kool-Aid probably developed a no-sugar version because _____**

A   it gives people a choice of the kind of Kool-Aid they want to buy

B   some people do not like Kool-Aid when it is too sweet

C   other drink companies were offering no-sugar versions

D   most children do not like sugar

Common Core Standard RL.4.3

☐ **Which words in the passage show that George Stephen believed in his new product?**

A   *Very daring at the time*

B   *Had the last laugh*

C   *Willingly spent*

D   *Took a lot of teasing*

Common Core Standard RL.4.3

☐ **Which sentence from the passage supports the idea that children often like the same foods as their parents?**

A   *These names are so familiar you probably have friends, parents, and grandparents who remember these products.*

B   *It is possible that Oreos have been eaten by as many as six generations in a single family.*

C   *It is true that some of these products have changed significantly to reflect the times.*

D   *Nevertheless, the black and white snack has been American's most popular cookie since its beginning, resulting in more than 450 billion consumed to date.*

Common Core Standard RL.4.3

☐ **Which words in the passage show that the box containing Barnum's Animal Crackers has not changed?**

A   *18 circus animals in each box*

B   *Not really crackers*

C   *8,000 miles of string are attached to the little boxes*

D   *Imported from England*

Common Core Standard RL.4.9

☐　　Based on information in the passage, which statement would *not* be reasonable?

A　　The Kool-Aid Man character was the inventor of the popular drink.

B　　Oreos are one of the most popular cookies on the market today.

C　　People drive long distances to find Krispy Kreme doughnuts because they have a reputation for being very tasty.

D　　It is possible that a nine year old child's grandfather ate Oreos when he was nine years old.

Common Core Standard RL.4.9

☐　　In paragraph 1, the author writes "the classics have survived the sands of   time" to show that these products _____

A　　taste good

B　　are no longer available

C　　are as popular now as they ever were

D　　have copied new products

Common Core Standard RL.4.9

☐　　After George Stephen's friends ate food prepared on the new kind of grill, they probably _____

A　　invited Mr. Stephen to their house for dinner

B　　volunteered to help him build the grills

C　　wanted him to cook more food

D　　wanted to buy a grill

Common Core Standard RL.4.2

☐   **This passage is mainly about _____**

A   strange foods that people eat

B   the anniversary of certain foods

C   how certain products got their names

D   products that have been on the market for between 50 and 120 years

---

Common Core Standard RL.4.2

☐   **The passage state that even parents and grandparents remember these products.   Tell in your own words how this could happen.**

_____

_____

_____

_____

_____

_____

_____

_____

Common Core Standard RL.4.2

☐   **People probably paid more for the Weber grill because _____**

A   George Stephen was a likeable man

B   the food tasted better than food prepared on other grills

C   the grill was different from other grills

D   the grill kept out rain

Common Core Standard RI.4.2

☐ This passage was written mainly to ____

A help readers know which kinds of cookies to buy

B inform readers about some well-known products that have been on the market for a very long time

C sell more of each kind of product that was discussed

D make the reader laugh

Common Core Standard RI.4.2

☐ The author probably included special sections giving facts about each product so ____

A the reader would have more to read

B people would want to learn more about old products

C the reader could learn about each product's history

D people would like the products

Common Core Standard RI.4.2

☐ The title of this passage, *Wonders of the Food World*, probably means ____

A questions about certain products

B very old products

C foods that taste good

D products that have caused surprise or admiration

Common Core Standard RL.4.6

☐   The author probably believes ____

A   these products should have been changed over the years

B   the Weber grill is the best kind of grill to buy

C   everyone's grandparents ate Oreos

D   these products are special and deserve our attention

Common Core Standard RL.4.6

☐   The author probably used humor when writing this passage so that ____

A   more people would read the passage

B   everyone would laugh

C   the reader could learn and also enjoy reading the selection

D   this passage would be different from other passages

Common Core Standard RL.4.6

☐   The author seems to believe that Oreos and a glass of milk can ____

A   cause someone to gain weight

B   enable someone to do a good job of thinking

C   answer many questions

D   solve problems

Common Core Standard RI.4.1, Common Core Standard RL.4.1

☐ **Which is a FACT in this passage?**

A   They taste good and appeal to many ages and cultures.

B   Before Karo light and dark corn syrups came into being in 1902, housewives had to take their syrup jugs to a store to be filled from barrels by a grocer.

C   It is not unusual for the younger set to introduce new versions of old favorites to their seniors.

D   However, George had the last laugh.

Common Core Standard RI.4.1, Common Core Standard RL.4.1

☐ **As soon as the Corn Products Refining Company began selling Karo syrup in containers to their customers, they _____**

A   named the syrup after the wife of an employee

B   created a waffle syrup

C   made a pecan pie called the Karo Pie

D   created a cookbook with recipes that used the syrup

Common Core Standard RI.4.1, Common Core Standard RL.4.1

☐ **Which of these is an OPINION in this passage?**

A   George Stephen's idea was daring at the time.

B   In the late 1950s, George Stephen bought the company.

C   This new cookie was baked by Nabisco, the National Biscuit Company.

D   Barnum's Animal Crackers were imported from England in the late 1800s.

Name _____

Common Core Standard RI.4.5, Common Core Standard RL.4.7

☐ **George Stephen wanted to make a barbecue grill with a lid so that** _____

A it would be more expensive than other grills

B it would have a dome shape

C the smoke would stay inside the grill and make the food taste better

D he could buy the company he worked for

Common Core Standard RI.4.1, Common Core Standard RL.4.1, Common Core Standard RL.4.7

☐ **Before the popular chocolate cookies were called Oreos, they were called** _____

A chocolate sandwiches

B biscuits

C black and white snacks

D cookies

Common Core Standard RI.4.1, Common Core Standard RL.4.1, Common Core Standard RL.4.7

☐ **Which is a FACT in this passage?**

A Today the light, shiny-frosted doughnuts have achieved nation-wide appeal.

B The easy answer is that they are all instant gratification.

C They are affordable, but high in quality and have widespread availability.

D Vernon Rudolph cut a hole in the wall and sold directly to his customers.

ANSWER KEY

THE LAUNDRY

Page 2	A, B, C
Page 3	B, D, A
Page 4	A, C, D
Page 5	A, B, D
Page 6	B, C, D
Page 7	C, B, A
Page 8	D, B, C
Page 9	B, D, A
Page 10	C, B, D
Page 11	A, C, B
Page 12	B, C, D
Page 13	D, A, B
Page 14	B, C, A
Page 15	B, D, C
Page 16	D, B, C
Page 17	B, C, B
Page 18	B, A, D
Page 19	B, D, C
Page 20	B, D, A
Page 21	A, B, D
Page 22	C, A, B

NELLIE BLY: A TRAVELING HERO

Page 25	B, A, C
Page 26	D, C, B
Page 27	C, A, D
Page 28	B, D, C
Page 29	C, B, D
Page 30	D, B, A
Page 31	C, B, D
Page 32	A, D, C
Page 33	D, C, A
Page 34	B, C, A
Page 35	C, A, B
Page 36	B, C, C
Page 37	C, B, D
Page 38	A, D, B
Page 39	A, C, D
Page 40	D, B, A
Page 41	D, A, C
Page 42	B, B, D
Page 43	C, C, B
Page 44	C, B, D
Page 45	A, C, B

SOPHIE AND THE MAGIC WATERING CAN / WHAT HAPPENED TO CHRISTMAS?

Page 48	C, B, A
Page 49	B, A, A
Page 50	D, A, A
Page 51	B, C, A

Page 52	B, C, Open
Page 53	B, D, C
Page 54	Open, D, A
Page 55	C, Open, B
Page 56	B, A, Open
Page 57	A, D, C
Page 58	Open, B, C
Page 59	Open, C, B
Page 60	C, A, A

THE LIFE OF A WHALE

Page 63	B, C, D
Page 64	A, B, C
Page 65	D, C, A
Page 66	C, B, A
Page 67	B, A, D
Page 68	B, C, C
Page 69	C, A, B
Page 70	C, A, D
Page 71	B, D, C
Page 72	D, D, B
Page 73	A, C, B
Page 74	B, D, C
Page 75	C, A, D
Page 76	A, D, B
Page 77	B, C, A
Page 78	C, B, A
Page 79	B, D, A
Page 80	D, D, C
Page 81	D, A, A
Page 82	A, C, B

WONDERS OF THE FOOD WORLD

Page 86	B, D, C
Page 87	A, D, C
Page 88	C, A, A
Page 89	B, B, D
Page 90	C, D, A
Page 91	D, B, C
Page 92	A, C, D
Page 93	D, Open, B
Page 94	B, C, D
Page 95	D, C, B
Page 96	B, D, A
Page 97	C, B, D

CPSIA information can be obtained at www.ICGtesting.com
Printed in the USA
LVOW09s2248250216

476771LV00026B/508/P